ROLAND-MICHEL BARRIN
DE LA GALISSONIÈRE

La Galissonière was the most remarkable of the governors of New France in the eighteenth century, although he spent only a short time there (1747 to 1749). He stood out above all through his intellectual qualities: his mind was brilliant, wide-ranging, and nourished by a creative imagination which was fertile in new ideas and rapid solutions.

Roland-Michel Barrin de la Galissonière was born at Rochefort, France, in November 1693. At 17 he joined the navy, and after a successful career was sent to Canada at the age of 54 as "commander-in-chief of the colony," at a time when it was in great peril. La Galissonière grasped the many problems quickly and clearly, and set out to restructure the colony, to join its badly fitting parts together in an organized whole. The attitude of his superiors at home was a major difficulty. Neither Vaudreuil nor Beauharnois, his predecessors, had been able to jolt the minister and the king out of their apathy concerning the colony; La Galissonière made the alarm they had sounded timidly ring out in the offices of Versailles. He attempted desperately the impossible recovery they had not known how to carry out in time.

This biographical essay paints a vivid and forceful picture of New France on the eve of the Seven Years' War.

CANON LIONEL GROULX, ordained a priest in June 1903, dedicated himself for forty years to teaching, in particular Canadian history. In 1946 he founded the Institut d'histoire de l'Amérique française and edited its journal from 1947 until his death. This volume is his last work.

Roland-Michel Barrin de La Galissonière

1693-1756

LIONEL GROULX

CANADIAN BIOGRAPHICAL STUDIES

UNIVERSITY OF TORONTO PRESS

CANADIAN BIOGRAPHICAL STUDIES

1 *John Strachan* 1778-1867, J. L. H. HENDERSON

2 *Roland-Michel Barrin de La Galissonière* 1693-1756,
LIONEL GROULX

© University of Toronto Press 1970

Reprinted in paperback 2017

ISBN 978-0-8020-3237-9 (cloth)

ISBN 978-1-4875-9930-0 (paper)

Foreword

The "Canadian Biographical Studies/Études biographiques canadiennes" series is a joint undertaking of the University of Toronto Press and the Presses de l'Université Laval. Since 1961 the two presses have collaborated closely in the editing and publication of the *Dictionary of Canadian Biography/Dictionnaire biographique du Canada*, with which this new series is intimately associated. During the work leading up to the publication of the first volumes of the DCB/DBC it became clear that although the leading figures in Canadian history have for the most part been the subject of good studies and are relatively well known to specialists and the general public, the same is not true, generally speaking, for the persons of lesser importance, and particularly for those who made their careers outside the realms of

politics and religion, in finance, industry, and trade or in
education, the fine arts, and literature. This series will
therefore strive particularly to give their due to these
often neglected makers of our history, to cast light upon
periods in their lives that are still little known, and to
evaluate their contribution to the society of their time;
we hope to make that time better known by describing
the environment in which they lived.

With this as their aim the studies published in this
series, though limited to about a hundred pages in length,
will gradually form a reservoir of information of all sorts
upon which the contributors to the *Dictionary of Canadian Biography/Dictionnaire biographique du Canada*
may draw. In addition they will provide for different
periods of our history and various regions of our country
indispensable details concerning the political, economic,
social, and religious context in which moved the persons
whose biographies will appear in the DCB/DBC. These
Canadian biographical studies will nevertheless exist in
their own right and have their own importance: while
being of use to the specialists they will, we hope, also be
appreciated by the general public for their literary qualities, as are the two volumes of the *Dictionary of Canadian
Biography/Dictionnaire biographique du Canada* already published. These works will be written by
leading experts and the best authors and will all be published in the two official languages of Canada.

It is not without a certain pride that the series in the French edition is inaugurated with the last work of the late Canon Lionel Groulx, who died at Vaudreuil (Quebec) on 23 May 1967 at 89 years of age. He had been invited to prepare it in the summer of 1966; he delivered it a few months before his death. Strictly speaking, the work is much more an essay on Roland-Michel Barrin de La Galissonière's colonial policy than a biographical study in the sense in which the term is applied to this series. The editors, nonetheless, came to the conclusion that even if it contains little purely biographical information, the study paints such a vivid and forceful picture of New France on the eve of the Seven Years' War that it should be retained in the series and be included as a rather unusual entry in it. We are confident that readers will approve of this decision, inasmuch as Canon Groulx's essay re-creates with great success the setting in which lived so many of the persons whose biographies will appear in the third and fourth volumes of the DCB/DBC and thus attains one of the main objects of the "Canadian Biographical Studies/Etudes biographiques canadiennes."

La Galissonière was the most remarkable of the governors of New France in the 18th century, although he spent only two years there (1747-49). Replacing La Jonquière temporarily, he succeeded Beauharnois (1726-47), who had taken over from Vaudreuil (1703-25). After 1713, the year of the Peace of Utrecht—a treaty ultimately

fatal to New France because of the grievous losses of
territory that it occasioned and the ambiguity of its provisions, of which the English were to take advantage – the
colony had enjoyed the longest period of peace in its history. It was an excellent opportunity for France to repair
the damage caused by this treaty of 1713 and undo its
most serious results, to consolidate her positions in
America at the same time preparing for the inevitable
assault by the English forces, and to restore while there
was still time a situation that was leading to disaster. But
France, who was more interested in Europe than in
America, pursued a policy on the Continent that was in-
compatible with her interests in America and provided
only grudgingly for the needs of her Canadian colony,
which, with much grumbling, she was content to let live
precariously. The colonies to the south, however, which
were at the height of their expansion, took advantage of
the vague stipulations of the Peace of Utrecht to spread
into French territories and entrench themselves there. At
the same time, yielding to the double attraction of geo-
graphy and trade, New France kept pushing forward her
frontiers, especially to the west. As the English extended
their territories they grew stronger; as the French did,
they grew weaker. Neither Vaudreuil nor Beauharnois,
both of whom were quite elderly and deficient in will,
jolted the minister and the king out of their apathy concerning the colony, as they should have; in Bourla-
maque's words, they were unable to adopt the "note of

truth so necessary for informing ministers about distant matters." La Galissonière was to make ring out forcibly in the offices in Versailles the alarm that they had sounded too timidly; he was to attempt desperately the "impossible recovery" that they had not known how to carry out in time.

ANDRÉ VACHON

The assistance of Professor John Flinn in the preparation of this study for publication in English is gratefully acknowledged. One of the translators of French texts of the DCB/DBC into English, he has also translated this related work.

The Canada Council has assisted the preparation of this edition.

Contents

ROLAND-MICHEL BARRIN DE LA GALISSONIÈRE

Introduction

History is not lacking in examples of men who, on the eve of catastrophes, appear on the scene and exert themselves to repair the irreparable. Quite the reverse of a Cassandra, rather, ardently given to action, they are acutely aware of what pessimists call fatality and despite it attempt to re-establish a situation that is beyond saving. Was La Galissonière* such a man?

Unquestionably he is a personage who has been too much forgotten, who has been neglected by history, which has not assigned him his proper place. Claude de Bonnault, in a short and also superficial biography, considered La Galissonière and Frontenac to be the two out-

---

* Many historians use the form La Galissonnière; however, La Galissonière himself signed his name with one *n*, which is the spelling adopted for this volume.

standing figures in the gallery of governors of New France.[1] If, despite his faults, Frontenac possessed the will to dominate, the gift of command, if not the panache of the leader, La Galissonière stood out above all through his intellectual qualities; his mind was brilliant, wide-ranging, nourished moreover by a creative imagination which was fertile in new ideas and rapid solutions. This man, whose rule lasted only two years, raised hopes for what might have been a turning point in the history of New France. What importance did our earlier historians accord him? Abbé Jean-Baptiste Ferland, who is so often given to recounting anecdotes, makes an effort to resume the principal features of the administration of the person whom he always calls the "Comte" de La Galissonière.[2] François-Xavier Garneau understood the man and his work: "He governed Canada for only two years; but in this short lapse of time he applied a strong stimulus to the administration and gave the ministers advice which, if it had been followed, might have secured France in possession of this fine colony."[3]

Who, then, was La Galissonière? We know too little about his early years. We do know, however, that his family, which came from Brittany, included in its ranks members of the *parlement*, intendants, great merchants, and, very close to him, highly placed officials, the Beauharnois, the Bégons. His own father had married a Bégon, Catherine, the daughter of Michel Bégon, the first of the dynasty. This La Galissonière, Roland Barrin, a sailor, ultimately became commander of a squadron and rear-admiral.[4] His son, Roland-Michel Barrin, was born at Rochefort, where his father was in command of the Marine, on 5 November 1693 – according to others, 10 or 11 November.[5] He too was to bear quite properly the title of marquis, even though in some official documents he is occasionally given the title of count. The La Galissonières' property, in the region of Nantes, had been raised to a marquisate in 1658.[6]

Young La Galissonière studied at the Collège de Beauvais in Paris under the guidance of Charles Rollin, an excellent innovator in teaching methods who was also the teacher of Charles de Secondat de Montesquieu and in a sense of Jean-Jacques Rousseau. Rollin did not fail to perceive La Galissonière's talents. A long friendship linked pupil and master. The pupil devoted himself ardently to the study of mathematics (in them he saw the principle of all the sciences necessary to a naval officer), although he did not neglect the learning and training useful to a military man.[7] At the age of 17 he entered the service as a midshipman. Three years later, having become a sub-lieutenant the previous year, he married Marie-Catherine-Antoinette de Lauzon, daughter of the seigneur of La Gonterie in Poitou, a member of the family of a former governor of Canada.[8] His career went ahead. In 1726 he was assistant-adjutant, in 1727 a lieutenant-commander; then he commanded the *Dromadaire*, the *Héros*, and warships bearing the names *Le*

Tigre, La Gloire, Le Saint-Michel,[9] in squadrons led by
Claude-Élisée de Court de la Bruyère and Jacques de
Roquefeuil, among others. In 1738 he was promoted
captain.[10]

It was not his first visit when he arrived in Canada in
1747. Before his voyage in 1739,[11] when he commanded
the king's ship *Le Rubis,*[12] he had already been at Quebec
at least eight times. At the ministry of the Marine he was
well thought of. In 1732 the minister, Jean-Frédéric
Phélypeaux de Maurepas, had written: "I was pleased
with the report that you gave me on the diligence and
ability of Monsieur de La Galissonière and of the other
officers and midshipmen who served on *Le Rubis.*"[13]

In 1747 war was raging in Europe, and had been since
the summer of 1744 when Louis xv had sided with
Prussia against Austria and England in what became the
War of the Austrian Succession. The French navy was
suffering one disaster after another. It was believed in
Paris that Pierre-Jacques de Taffanel de La Jonquière,
who had been sent to Canada to replace the governor,
Charles Beauharnois de La Boische, had been defeated
at sea and taken prisoner by the English. In New France
the situation was disturbing. New England was increasing its pressure. The king and the minister turned to La
Galissonière. Maurepas and Louis xv stated without
ambiguity the reasons for their choice: "The greatest
help, however, the one that the colony most needs at this

time, is a head who is capable of leading and defending it"[14]

La Galissonière had just reached the age of 54. It may be presumed that he was at the height of his powers. He was rather short and even "slightly deformed," according to Peter Kalm,[15] but anyone who has seen his portrait has been struck by the shrewdness of this face and its expression of serenity and quiet energy.

1 *A Colony in Danger*

La Galissonière arrived in Canada on 19 September
1747 on board a vessel which had been captured from the
English, the *Northumberland*. He did not bear the title
of governor, which remained M. de La Jonquière's. He
was "commander-in-chief of the colony," but with the
same power, the same authority, the right to the same
prerogatives, the same honours, the same emoluments as
a governor.

The new arrival was able immediately to measure the
difficulty and immensity of his task. The colony was in
the middle of a crisis. Its stronghold, Louisbourg, had
been lost to the English; all attempts to recapture it had
failed; Acadia was also lost, and Cape Breton Island,
which it was difficult to supply, was menaced; the Gulf of
St Lawrence was infested by English privateers who car-

ried on their operations right into the river. In the heart of New France the situation was equally distressing: people lived under the threat of an invasion by the English via Lake Champlain, the Richelieu, and the St Lawrence. As in the worst days, a system of signals had been set up on Beauharnois' orders along the St Lawrence; the settlers had also received instructions to evacuate the country before the enemy and to prepare hiding places in the woods. To cap it all, the alliance with the Indians, indispensable for the defence of New France, was proving to be more than shaky. The intrigues of the English and the Iroquois, the rumours which were adroitly spread about concerning France's naval reverses, had borne fruit; and to confirm those rumours, there were the posts in the interior, the *pays d'en-haut*, which as a result of the war were deprived of goods and were incapable of meeting the Indians' needs or supplied them only with merchandise of inferior quality. Moreover, as another result of the war, the colony was faced with a real financial crisis. As ships were prevented from coming from France, supplies were no longer arriving; the warehouses in Montreal and Trois-Rivières were almost empty; as a result, prices and salaries were going up and the king was reluctant to support the currency of the country. At his wits' end, the poor intendant, Gilles Hocquart, begged the minister to save his administration from ending in such a way.[1] Finally, on all the frontiers of the colony, in Acadia, in Canada, about the Great Lakes, towards the

Ohio and Mississippi, pressure was being exercised by the English and was steadily becoming stronger and more cunning. Never had a new governor, unless perhaps Frontenac during his second term of administration, confronted a situation that was so seriously jeopardized, so critical.

We might well wonder at the rapidity of La Galisso-nière's reactions to the problem facing him. He grasped it quickly and clearly. He complained, we know, that he had not been able to get information as speedily as he would have desired and of having left France "very ill-informed about the affairs of the country," and he reached Canada after a crossing that had been too long. This was the complaint of a prudent man who did not want to reach a decision until he knew what he was doing. The fact remains that upon his arrival and during the months that followed he himself experienced the anxi-eties of the colony. Like everyone else, he expected an invasion. He was also able to talk with Beauharnois be-fore he sailed, which was not until 14 October 1747. Above all, he was able to discuss the affairs of the colony with Hocquart, who extended his stay in Canada by a few weeks. The commander-in-chief put these conversations to good use, even though he admitted at times that he was not in agreement with the intendant.[2] He was also able to obtain information from Honoré Michel de Villebois de La Rouvillière, the commissary at Montreal.[3] Until the end of his administration he was to have, besides, his own

ways of obtaining information on all matters. Kalm
describes him to us, questioning *voyageurs*, missionaries,
commandants of posts passing through Quebec or Montreal, concerning the regions from which they came.[4] To
gain knowledge about the West he sent two engineers,
the Sieur Gaspard-Joseph Chaussegros de Léry, to Michilimackinac, and the Sieur Michel Chartier de Lotbinière,
to Detroit, "to observe everything that may be useful to
the service and to draw up reports on it." Father Joseph-
Pierre de Bonnecamps, who was to accompany Pierre-
Joseph de Céloron de Blainville on a voyage to the Ohio,
was not sent for any other purpose.[5] What bears La Galissonière's stamp in all these measures was the use he made
of this mass of information and the broad, composite view
that he took of the problem of New France. One might
have thought that Jean Talon had come back to Canada.
But there was much more to be done than in Talon's
time. Since 1672 horizons had become broader; the task
had become significantly greater. What Talon had only
dreamt of, had a presentiment of, La Galissonière saw, at
least in part, being realized.

His work, we would say today, was the "restructuring"
of the French empire in North America, the joining
together into an organized whole its badly fitting parts.
La Galissonière – optimism itself – was going to undertake this task despite the state of crisis which prevailed.
Of little importance to him, it seems, were the obstacles
of all sorts that he was to encounter: first and foremost

the lack of vigour or the waverings of the king's colonial policy and the torpor that reigned in the offices at Versailles and Paris. As far as the king was concerned, La Galissonière hoped to give him faith in his colonies. As for the offices, he would not hesitate to shake them up. Of this man of action Jean-Paul Granjean de Fouchy, his panegyrist, was to say with great justice: "Like Caesar, he thought he had done nothing from the moment that he could do something more."[6]

La Galissonière would have liked first of all to retake the parts of the empire that had been lost: Acadia and Hudson Bay. In a memorandum from the king intended for La Jonquière's information and dated 1 April 1746, Acadia is mentioned as already being no longer part of the French possessions. His Majesty described New France thus: "It comprises Canada and Louisiana, with their dependencies."[7] All hope of retaking Louisbourg and Acadia was, however, not lost. That was even one of the instructions given to the ill-starred squadron under the command of the Duc d'Anville. The defeat which befell the squadron did not prevent brilliant exploits from being performed in the Acadian peninsula. In February 1747 a detachment of 300 Canadians and Indians under the command of Nicolas-Antoine Coulon de Villiers, who was replaced in the heat of action by the Chevalier Louis-Luc de La Corne, obliged a strongly entrenched English force, which was half as strong again as the attackers, to surrender. It was a day marked by heroic actions. To have been present at Minas became a title to fame and even the best recommendation for obtaining the king's favours.[8] Neither Beauharnois nor Hocquart, therefore, nor even the king resigned themselves to the loss of Louisbourg and Acadia, "this lovely and fertile province" as it is called in a dispatch of the period.[9]

It is consequently understandable that, immediately upon his arrival, La Galissonière cast his eyes in that direction. He was well aware that the English considered Louisbourg "as another Dunkirk which would always keep them at arm's length."[10] On becoming the masters of the fortress of Louisbourg they had become the masters of fishing and trading along the coasts of all the surrounding region; they could acquire the monopoly of dried fish in Europe. The port offered shelter to their ships. From then on, indeed, Beauharnois and Hocquart had guessed England's plans, aimed at seizing all the strategic passages or points on the seas: Louisbourg, Antigua, Jamaica, Gibraltar, Port Mahon. La Galissonière had been able to learn that the fate of Louisbourg and that of Acadia were inseparably linked: it was impossible to keep Louisbourg without keeping Acadia; it was impossible to retake Acadia without retaking Louisbourg. Beauharnois and Hocquart even went so far as to maintain that the future of Canada was at stake.[11] "Holding on to Canada must be considered the most important aim; once the enemy were to become master of it [Acadia], it would perhaps be necessary to give up this continent forever."[12]

Nothing more was needed for La Galissonière to take to heart the problem of Acadia which was, in short, the problem of the maritime route to Canada, the respiratory tract which, if it were blocked, would bring about the asphyxiation of the colony.

The peace of 1748, which was called "patched up" in Europe and which gave rise to the expression *bête comme la paix* ("as stupid as the peace"), was no less "patched up" in Canada. It restored everything as it had been before the war. What was unfortunate for Acadia was, in effect, that since the Treaty of Utrecht there had been no agreement upon what was called Acadia. It was a geographical reality which raised a host of thorny questions. For the English, Acadia, "according to its former frontiers," extended well beyond the isthmus; it extended into the bordering mainland and took in the Abenakis' country (Maine). For La Galissonière, Acadia, "according to its former frontiers," was nothing but the Acadian peninsula, with its boundary formed by the isthmus. He maintained that of all the maps printed in England "none that I have seen has yet carried the fraud to the point of applying the name of Acadia to territory beyond the peninsula." La Galissonière consequently protested vigorously against the neighbour's encroachments: "Even before learning that peace had been concluded," he wrote, they had begun to push forward towards lands that "belong unquestionably to Canada" (in particular the territory of the Saint John River), and that were already

inhabited by French settlers. The claims of the English
went so far, he insisted, that to accede to them would be
tantamount to giving up "all communications by land
between Canada and Acadia and Cape Breton Island, and
all means of succouring the one and retaking the other."
The English were also arrogating to themselves all the
coast from the Saint John River to Beaubassin (Chig-
necto), "from Canso to Gaspé," including the interior of
the country, which would make them the masters of the
territory of the Abenaki tribe, who had always been loyal
to the French, and of several posts on the Gulf of St
Lawrence, in short "a territory that comprises more than
180 leagues of coast, that is to say almost as much as from
Bayonne to Dunkirk." La Galissonière, who was always
ready to go into action, warned Maurepas that "if it is
desired to prevent this country from being split, measures must be taken in Europe to stop the undertakings of
the English."[13]

He had not waited for the minister's authorization to
take some highly significant measures. He had, for example, forbidden the Abenakis to take the oath of loyalty
that the English were demanding of them.[14] He had sent
Charles Deschamps, Sieur de Raffetot et de Boishébert,
with a small detachment off in the direction of the Saint
John River to reassure the settlers. He was not, he said,
the first governor of Canada since the Treaty of Utrecht
to claim these lands. Previously they had been claimed
as belonging to the Abenakis; he was claiming them as

French territory, without, however, relinquishing any part of the other claim.[15]

There remained another territory that La Galissonière would have liked to recapture, and that was Hudson Bay. He was aware of the extraordinary trade in beaver pelts that was carried on there; and these beaver pelts, the finest in America, came, according to him, from lands which belonged to the king of France. Significantly, the minister, in his dispatch in 1746 in which he had instructed Beauharnois to limit himself to essential operations as an economy measure, nevertheless recommended that the governor risk a raid, if possible, in the Hudson Bay region, in preference even to "other objectives."[16] La Galissonière did not discard these instructions. He had prepared a raid for the spring of 1749, but the signing of peace put an end to his project.[17] This plan illustrates the commander-in-chief's firm determination to wipe out all the harmful consequences of the Treaty of Utrecht. In his "Mémoire sur les colonies de la France dans l'Amérique septentrionale" in 1750, for example, he maintained that since the Treaty of Utrecht spoke only of "restitution," and since the English had never had any settlement within reach of the sea, it followed that "the interior of the country is deemed to belong to France." Therefore, only force could take Hudson Bay from the English, at the next outbreak of war.[18]

For the moment other tasks called him elsewhere. All the frontiers of New France appeared to him to be poorly established or breached. On all sides the claims of the English adversary were being pushed, often accompanied by violations of French territory. Convinced that the end of the French in Canada was near, the English were taxing their ingenuity to extend and consolidate their encroachments. Consequently La Galissonière undertook to strengthen New France's long chain of fortifications. He would give his attention to the construction of Fort Saint-Jean on the Richelieu River. The Richelieu and Lake Champlain were natural invasion routes. They had been the route preferred by the Iroquois, as they would be by the English. Besides, the latter claimed the Lake Champlain region as part of their territory.[19] La Galissonière retorted that these claims were unfounded and recalled the fact that the lake had been discovered by Samuel de Champlain. Moreover, this region had been for a time a centre of lumbering operations by the French. They had even built there, without encountering any protests, Fort Saint-Frédéric (Crown Point, NY), which was intended to protect the neighbouring seigneuries – some fifteen, according to the engineer Louis Franquet.[20] Plans for a second fort, Saint-Jean, throw light on the idea behind La Galissonière's vast programme: to build at all the vital points in the colony posts or forts which would constitute powerful pivotal points designed to command and protect a whole region. The role of Fort Saint-Jean, built above all the rapids on the Richelieu, was to serve as a cover for Fort Saint-Frédéric, an advanced sentinel to the south. It also facilitated lumbering operations and the installing of settlers on the lands around Lake Champlain. Thanks to a road which reached as far as La Prairie de la Magdeleine (Laprairie), Montreal could send aid to Saint-Frédéric within 48 hours. With the elimination of the deviation through Chambly a saving of 6,000 *livres* a year was made in transportation costs.[21]

La Galissonière looked more attentively towards the West, towards that immense extension of the empire which, via the St. Lawrence and the Ottawa Rivers, stretched as far as the Great Lakes, then, via the lakes, to the Illinois country and Louisiana.

The West! The *pays d'en-haut*! Had anyone ever formed a true picture of the seething, intricate life vibrating at that time in this immense area? Indian tribes which were all called "Ottawas" but which varied in features, numbers, customs, lived there side by side or widely dispersed. They travelled, they met in the woods or on the lakes. The missionaries had christianized and civilized them superficially. But they had not lost their hereditary background completely. They had remained unruly in character. Thefts, murders, crimes of all sorts were not unusual among them. They had kept their liking for manhunts and for internecine warfare. They had also acquired some of the white man's vices, in particular unchastity and alcoholism. For in this environment lived, widely scattered also, *voyageurs*, fur-traders, leaders of posts and their soldiers. The West was, in fact, a province, or even an organic part of the empire. There was the storehouse of furs, the harvest that had to be reaped every year and that supplied, or close to it, the only article of exchange for the goods from Europe. The richer the harvest was, the more firmly established became the well-being, if not the prosperity, of the colony and of its trade, its land-clearing operations, its small industries.

In these vast territories, the military post, with its stockade and sometimes its little fort, on the lakes or in the surrounding area bore witness to the presence of France and to its sovereignty. As the representative of authority the leader of the post was held responsible for the *Pax indiana*. He had to settle disputes between the tribes and prevent their local wars. He was a peace-maker; he was just as much an officer who was responsible for administering justice and law among the Indians as well as between the Indians and the French. For, wherever there were dissensions and disorders the Indian stopped hunting, and the harvest in furs was reduced. This harvest also had to be defended against smuggling and against the intrigues of the Iroquois, which were carried on for the benefit of the English merchants. An increase in the price of French merchandise or a decline in quality – which happened too frequently because of the niggardliness of the merchants in France – were enough to set off smuggling to Oswego (NY).

What qualities were required of the leader or com-

mander of a post? Left to his own resources most of the
time, too far away to be able to refer matters to the au-
thorities, he could only rely on his instructions, but
particularly on his tact, his diplomatic sense, his honesty,
his energy, and, inevitably, on his prestige with the Indians and the French. The true post leader was, in reality,
a little governor and a little intendant in his region. Rare
were the men capable of playing this difficult role. And
yet La Galissonière was to apply himself to discovering
them, while at the same time he devoted his energies to
establishing the truly strategic posts or to fortifying them.

   There too, in this region of the West, of vital importance to New France, pressure from the English was grow-
ing. La Galissonière considered this pressure particularly
threatening at Oswego, south of Lake Ontario. Because of
its very situation, how much concern this English enclave
was to cause him! He saw in it the yawning gap in his plan
of fortifications, or if one prefers, the sharp sword capable
of cutting New France in two. As soon as Oswego had
been built, Beauharnois had protested vigorously against
what he considered to be a flagrant encroachment. La
Galissonière's reaction was no less violent. "If this fort
remains in the hands of the English when peace is established, it will be an eternal source of strife and a sure and
permanent means for our enemies to entice away our
Indians." Why did the French limit themselves to protest-
ing, he was to write later, when a large part of the furs from
the West were escaping from them through Oswego,

often by means of the French themselves, many of whom were engaged in smuggling.[22] The disappearance of Oswego was of such importance to him that he would have been willing to exchange Fort George (Lake George, NY) for Oswego, even though this other fort also seemed to him to be an encroachment.[23] He was obliged, however, to admit that it was impossible to capture Oswego except with forces superior to the enemy's and with the Iroquois' assent. This did not prevent him from coming close to risking the adventure. He hoped to win over the Iroquois or else intimidate them. But the presents which the English gave their faithful Iroquois allies, and above all the peace of 1748, brought everything to nought.[24]

It was, nevertheless, essential to fortify, and more strongly than elsewhere if possible, the immense turntable which was constituted by the other Great Lakes. If it is kept in mind that the following description is found in letters from the period of September 1747 to September 1748, it can be realized how much accurate information La Galissonière acquired in a short time on the vast western region. There was, first of all, Niagara (Niagara Falls, Ont.), at the junction of Lake Ontario and Lake Erie, in the vicinity of the Iroquois tribes. In this place and in its wretched fort La Galissonière had immediately detected, in the words of a commandant whom he sent there, "one of the keys of the country." And how right he was! At that time Niagara was the point of passage be-

tween east and west, and consequently the route followed by the Indians from the *pays d'en-haut* on their
way to Oswego,Orange (Albany, NY), and Boston, and,
in the other direction, the route which allowed the English and Iroquois to take their merchandise to the Indians
of the Lakes and to stir them up against the French.
Surrounded by hostile tribes, moreover, under constant
threat of attack, the fort at Niagara, tottery on the whole,
was, of all those in the West, least in a position to be
succoured. The peace of 1748 would have afforded the
possibility of postponing repairs. Clear-sighted as he was,
La Galissonière meant to make the fort secure against all
surprises as quickly as possible.[25]

Niagara was, in fact, the passage to what was generally
called the *pays d'en-haut*. These territories abounded in
military posts, trading posts, fortified or not, and forts
where trade was also carried on. The posts in the north
had to be distinguished from those in the south, all of
them pivoting upon bigger ones which were taking on
the appearance of small capitals. Included in the posts to
the south, pivoting on Detroit, were the posts among the
Illinois, the Miamis of the Cuyahoga River, and the
Ouyatanons or Wabash nations; those on Green Bay,
Lake Superior, and the *"Mer de l'Ouest"* were counted
among the posts in the north; that on the St. Joseph
River could be attached to either group.[26]

A problem arose: which should be the capital of the
southern posts? Obviously the post that could subsist

almost entirely by itself and at the same time defend all
the others within its reach. This post could be no other
than Detroit, at the junction of the southern and northern lakes. For many years, since the time of Antoine
Laumet de Lamothe de Cadillac, thought had been given
to establishing Detroit on foundations that would have
some chance of enduring. When Deschamps de Boishébert arrived there in 1732 he found the settlement "very
little advanced for having been begun more than 30 years
ago."[27] Detroit had to be settled with a great number of
farm labourers, he said, to whom, in order to contribute
to advancing settlement, might be handed over all the
profits which could be made from the post. For his part,
La Galissonière believed that a strong settlement at Detroit would prevent "disturbances" among the Indians
of the *pays d'en-haut*. This post would, furthermore, shut
the English out of the lakes, even preventing them from
settling on the Ohio River.[28] He drew a sort of compari-
son between Detroit and the posts in the Illinois country.
In the latter region the climate and the land were better,
and the Indians were more loyal and tractable. On the
other hand, trade in pelts was more profitable and easier
at Detroit, but the Indians were more prone to be de-
bauched. The Illinois posts consisted only of a series of
small stations "isolated" from one another. Detroit, however, could not and would not long remain "in one
piece."[29] After his return to France La Galissonière came
back to the question of Detroit in his report in 1750.

He would have liked to instal a thousand farmers as settlers there. No other site in the interior of Canada was more suitable for the founding of a town which would be better situated to attract all the trade on the lakes. In addition, with its strong garrison and its population, it would inspire respect in all the Indians, it would protect the Ohio and Mississippi regions and even the posts situated north of the lakes.[30]

The capital of the northern posts still had to be decided upon. Again the site appeared to be clearly indicated: Michilimackinac, the former centre of the Ottawa missions, a stopping point for *voyageurs* going up to the head of the lakes or down via the Ottawa. There was one obstacle, the continual scarcity of meat and "of a thousand other things that would be considered necessities in France." Nevertheless, thought La Galissonière, until a better place turned up this was the obvious choice. A year later La Jonquière and François Bigot were to regret that settlers had not been brought in at Michilimackinac as at Detroit. The truth of the matter was that the poor quality of the soil was not conducive to such a policy.[31]

In choosing these posts La Galissonière wrestled in his mind with one problem: to what little capital, to which part of the empire should the Illinois posts be joined? To Detroit, that is to say to Canada? To Louisiana? The discussion had been going on for some time. The Illinois country, which had been opened by *voyageurs* from Canada, had remained a Canadian colony until 1717. Then, at the wish of the Compagnie d'Occident, which wanted to extend its trading operations, the Illinois country was transferred to Louisiana. As we have seen, the country was in reality made up only of small, scattered settlements. During his trip in 1721, however, Pierre-François-Xavier de Charlevoix discovered at Kaskaskia "a large village of Frenchmen, nearly all of them Canadians, who have a Jesuit as their priest."[31] And on that subject, who does not remember the enthusiastic description which Jacques Marquette and Louis Jolliet, on their way to the discovery of the Mississippi, gave of the Illinois country? What would have become of this Illinois country if, instead of wasting his energy on some barren islands in the Lower St. Lawrence, Jolliet, a man of action, had had the good fortune to obtain at that time this domain that he had asked for? One will also recall Charlevoix's descriptions in his *Journal historique*: "Impossible to find a better or more beautiful country ... All one sees are immense grasslands, strewn with small clumps of trees ... grasslands which stretch for 25 leagues."[33] And everywhere, even in its most remote regions, the country bore French names which indicated to what point *voyageurs* and *coureurs de bois* had left their mark on it.

At all events, La Galissonière, who was busy setting up his system of fortifications, had to decide whether the Illinois country would go to Canada or Louisiana. Pierre de Rigaud de Vaudreuil, who was at that time in

Louisiana, wanted to retain the Illinois forts under his
jurisdiction. To transfer them to Canada, he maintained,
would inflict a "deep wound" on his colony to the south,
without being of the slightest advantage to Canada; the
operation would even be fatal to the Illinois posts.
Louisiana, which was still not firmly established and
whose commerce was little developed, needed to supply
itself from as large a network as possible of surrounding
regions. Vaudreuil also brought up the matter of
distances. Being about 350 miles from New Orleans, but
800 leagues from the Canadian colony, the Illinois posts
could not have much hope for help from the St. Lawrence
valley, nor could they easily deliver their wares there,
which consisted entirely of bulky pelts. On the other
hand, New Orleans could receive from the Illinois posts
bear oil, tallow, ham, various kinds of meal, the products
of the fur trade, and lead extracted from mines which
were said to be rich, although little worked. Therefore,
concluded Vaudreuil, it was important that, to protect
their trade on the Mississippi, the banks of which were
inhabited by often hostile tribes, the Illinois posts should
be allowed to keep their companies of troops instead of
the simple little detachment they were being promised
from Canada. These companies were even necessary to
keep in order the inhabitants, who were sufficiently
numerous not to fear the Indians, and especially since
they were in large part *coureurs de bois* and *métis,*

"people refractory to discipline," whom the commandant of the Illinois posts had been able to keep in order up till then only by showing great firmness.[34]

La Galissonière had already given his opinion about the Illinois country on 1 September 1748. He had done so in his clear-sighted and precise manner. One should expect neither too much nor too little of this country. There was little to be hoped for from its mines and pelts, returns from which were mediocre. Yet it was a productive country and one that could be settled easily. It would perhaps be possible to tame the buffalo which swarmed over the region and to turn them into draught-oxen. Some use might be made of their hair, and especially it might be possible, by raising these animals, to set up a curing industry which would enable Martinique and the Spanish colonies to do without the "Irish cattle." In addition, bread, meat, and other foodstuffs produced there could not help but attract the Indians who were allied to the French, as well as their trade, which was so useful.[35] However, and once again we discover La Galissonière's overriding idea, this country deserved to be settled because of its strategic value. No barrier was better situated to prevent the English from penetrating into the French colonies and even into Mexico. If during the recent war, La Galissonière again stated forcefully, there had been four or five hundred men in the Illinois posts capable of bearing arms, not only would the small posts on the Wabash and elsewhere not have been disturbed, but the French could have led right into the heart of the English colonies the very Indian tribes that had insulted them. It was, nevertheless, up to Canada to undertake the task of settling this Illinois region. Louisiana lacked people itself and could not take it on. Besides, because of the difficulty of navigation on the Mississippi and the presence of too many hostile tribes along its banks, Louisiana was obliged to procure its flour from regions that were closer than the Illinois country.[36]

Another immense region, the valley of the Ohio, was causing serious concern. There, as elsewhere, the English were hastening to settle and to entrench themselves. The Ohio, which flowed into the Wabash and thence into the Mississippi, belonged to France, along with all its territory, in La Galissonière's view. This was in accord with the jurisprudence of the time. The Ohio was, in addition, particularly valuable strategically. As it was navigable for its whole length, this river opened up a broad route towards the southern basin of the Mississippi, and even towards Mexico. An English settlement on the Ohio, wrote La Galissonière in 1749, would give the enemy "access to all our posts and would open up [to him] the way to Mexico."[37] The English were already trading in these regions. The rumour had spread that very year that they were going to set up a post there. La Galissonière knew that he was on the eve of his departure: as soon as La Jonquière was liberated, he would have to sail for France. It seems that La Galissonière did not want to leave a single gap in the endless line of fortifications that was to enclose the colony. He had sent Deschamps de Boishébert off to the Saint John River. He dispatched to the Great Lakes, but first to the Ohio, one of the most remarkable officers of the period, Céloron de Blainville, sending with him to serve as chaplain, or rather to aid him, Father Joseph-Pierre de Bonnecamps, a mathematician and teacher of hydrography at the Jesuit college in Quebec. La Galissonière was convinced that Bonnecamps would bring back "more exact and detailed information than we have had up until now of those countries and of those through which the detachment will pass on its way there and back."[38] In point of fact, the French were rather late in paying attention to the Ohio. La Salle had discovered this river. There had been no attempt to make any settlements there, for fear of facilitating smuggling in beaver furs between the English and French. But La Galissonière considered that the Ohio was as harmful as Oswego. There, even more easily than at Oswego, the English could entice the Indian allies away from the French; likewise they could cut all connections between Canada and Louisiana; with moderately large forces, nothing would prevent them from threatening the posts in the Illinois country, all those on the Mississippi, those among the Miamis, and even Mexico.[39] Céloron set off, therefore, with a detachment of 200 Frenchmen and 30 Indians. He took with him men who were familiar with the region: Claude-Pierre Pécaudy de Contrecœur,

Augustin Legardeur de Courtemanche, Pierre-Roch de Saint-Ours, Coulon de Villiers, Joseph-Claude Boucher de Niverville.[40] Céloron's mission was important: he was to go part way down the Ohio, drive out the Hurons who had murdered some Frenchmen, remind some other Indians of their duty, and, above all, drive away the English who were coming to trade in these regions and were trying to establish themselves there. Finally, he was to take possession again of the Ohio and choose sites for possible settlements.[41]

Certainly Céloron's mission came just in time, if not too late. The entire Ohio region was in turmoil. As soon as Céloron's expedition was known, 300 Englishmen spread out through the villages to stir up the Indians. "The French," they told them, "are coming to the Ohio country to expel you from it." They brought in 40 horses laden with presents, sabres, bullets, gunpowder, even swivel-guns and mortars, which were distributed without charge among more than 70 Indian villages. The English were even supposed to have built three forts in different places and to have promised the Indians that they would defend them against the French emissary. On 3 September 1749, according to Father Bonnecamps, Englishmen transporting 40 packs of beaver furs were encountered on the Ohio, a hundred leagues from Philadelphia. And not only on the Ohio, but everywhere between it and Lake Erie the French detachment met Englishmen mingling with the Indians. Everywhere, too, the Indians exhibited either hostility or reserve. Some of them went so far as to hoist the English flag beside the French one.[42] The rumour had even spread that an attempt was being made to stir up a general rebellion of the Indians against the French in the *pays d'en haut*. The Ottawas and the Potawatomis at Detroit had refused in advance to join the French expedition.[43]

Céloron went ahead nonetheless with taking possession of the Ohio. The little ceremony took place on 29 August 1749. He had a lead plaque buried on the south bank of the Ohio, and the king's arms were fastened to a tree. When his party had passed the forty-first parallel of latitude they buried another lead plaque, near a large rock which was decorated with pictograms. Three other lead plaques were subsequently buried along their route. Finally, Céloron buried the sixth and last plaque on the west bank of the Great Miami River, north of the Ohio. Father Bonnecamps was nevertheless to have cause to jot down on one of the final pages of his journal this pessimistic remark: "There they are, then, the English, already deep in our territory, and, what is worse, they are there under the protection of a multitude of Indians whom they have drawn over to their side and whose number is increasing every day; their intent is doubtless not to stop there, and if adequate measures are not taken as quickly as possible to arrest their progress, we run a great risk of finding ourselves driven out shortly from the

pays d'en-haut and of being compelled to confine ourselves within the limits which it will please these gentle-
men to lay down for us. This is perhaps truer than one
imagines."[44] These were alarming reports, which La
Galissonière could not be informed of. The events which
Father Bonnecamps was relating took place at the end of
September 1749. At that time La Galissonière was on the
high seas, on his way to France.

One last gap, an extensive one, existed, then, between
Lake Erie and the Ohio. Would La Galissonière have
undertaken to close it? It must be repeated that he lacked
time to complete a task which, because it was carried out
too quickly, could not fail to bear the stamp of improvi-
sation. One must, all the same, pay homage to this man of
action for what he did accomplish and particularly for the
idea that he had conceived of his task. He had not reacted
purely as a soldier, imagining only a series of posts in the
wilds, widely separated, without any sign of the presence
of the French or of French might other than a stockade
and a flag floating above the walls. La Galissonière had
really wanted the West to be settled. He had wanted all
the pivotal points of the empire to be alive, strong, sus-
tained by real people. He had advocated for Fort Saint-
Frédéric, for example, the creation of "a big, strongly
fortified French village."[45] First of all, the population of
the colony had to be reinforced at all costs. The number
of settlements was increasing, some of them even close to

the English. Garrisons were essential in places where
formerly there had been no need of them. Since the war
the need for defence had been met by flying bands of
Canadians and Indians: this entailed costs which kept
increasing and was detrimental to both groups, as the
Canadians no longer wanted to farm and the Indians,
well fed and well clothed, lost their interest in hunting.
It was preferable, therefore, to bring the companies of
colonial regular troops up to strength each year with fre-
quent recruiting. Many soldiers, La Galissonière had
observed, married and became good settlers, while still
remaining good soldiers if need arose. If such a policy had
been practised earlier, it would have supplied the means
of containing the enemy.[46]

La Galissonière wanted this reinforcing of the population to be extended to the posts in the Illinois country. He
seems to have received reliable information from an intelligent officer who had a command there, the Chevalier de
Bertet,[47] to the effect that of all the colonies in New
France the Illinois country was the one that the English
could most easily infiltrate, and do so with small forces. It
was therefore urgent to furnish this colony with more
settlers. La Galissonière laid forth his plan, then, which
provided for sending immediately a detachment of 50 to
60 soldiers and 2 officers from Canada, and the return to
Louisiana of the two companies that were then on the
spot, although those soldiers who were already married
were to be retained; 30 to 40 salt-traders were to

be sent to the Illinois posts every year; in addition, each year the transfer from Canada to the Illinois posts of 12 to 15 settlers who were desirous of taking up land there was to be encouraged; finally, the garrison of this colony was to be brought up as quickly as possible to 100 men and the commanding officer was to be instructed particularly to induce people to take up farming rather than the fur trade. La Galissonière attached such importance to peopling the Illinois posts that he went so far as to write to the minister that if the enemy was successful in slipping in between Louisiana and Canada, "the loss of the Mississippi and the ruin of Canada's internal trade would be certain, and the Spanish colonies, even Mexico, would be in very great danger."[48]

He advocated the same policy of increasing the number of settlers for Detroit, Michilimackinac, and the Ohio country. At all costs, he wrote, the English on the one hand had to be prevented from settling on the Ohio, and on the other the area had to be developed. But nothing would contribute more effectively to the realization of the latter aim than "to give up for some years the profit made from the post in favour of the settlers who want to take up land there."[49] La Galissonière lost no time in acting. In 1749 he sent some families "amounting to about 45 persons" to Detroit; the Sieur Charles de Sabrevois de Bleury, who took over there from the Chevalier Paul-Joseph Le Moyne de Longueuil, received, wrote La Galissonière, "the instructions which seemed to me the

most appropriate for increasing this settlement."[50] But
when Father Bonnecamps, who was with Céloron's party,
went through Detroit the following spring, he met the
settlers who had arrived there from Canada the preceding
year. Most of them had been content to eat the rations
distributed by the king; some of them had even gone to
seek their fortune elsewhere. And yet, Father Bonnecamps compared Detroit to Touraine and Beauce in
France, with its immense plains which were suitable for
wheat and needed only to be farmed, and its mild climate
(with scarcely two months of winter), which allowed the
same fruits to be grown as in France.[51]

If La Galissonière had still been in Canada, he would
Detroit, young Sabrevois de Bleury, the favourite of
Madame Michel Bégon (Élisabeth Rocbert de La Morandière), for his lack of ability and initiative. It was she who
had chosen him and had recommended him warmly to
La Galissonière.[52] How La Galissonière had the post at
Detroit at heart! It was to it, he was to say, "that the greatest attention must be paid today. If ever there were a
thousand farmers settled in this district, it would feed and
defend all the others. Of the whole of the interior of
Canada it is the most suitable place for founding a town
where all the trade of the Lakes would concentrate and
which, if supplied with a good garrison and surrounded
by a good number of settlers' farms, would be in a situation to impose respect on nearly all the Indians on the
continent."[53]

Why, one wonders, was there not an advocacy of massive immigration, as in Talon's time? La Galissonière did, in fact, recommend this policy in his "Memoire" in 1750. At that time he asserted that the decision had to be made "to send many people to New France in order to enable those who are in charge of administering it to apply themselves at the same time to the various settlements that have been proposed." He also wrote, with reference to Canada: "No effort must be spared to make these colonies strong, since we can and must consider them as the bulwark in America against the enterprises of the English."[54]

Had La Galissonière forgotten the Indian allies in all this? He was quite aware of their role in the system of fortifications in New France. In a colony with too small a population the Indians had always constituted, even more than the forts, the trump card, and had turned out to be indispensable auxiliaries. It is true that a price had to be paid. These allies cost dearly in arms and rations. But how was one to do without them? In a war fought in the woods they showed unmatched flair, since they knew the paths and routes, could follow a man's track as easily as that of a wild beast, were capable of fighting with ardour and of risking everything for a scalp; at the same time they were fickle-minded allies who served and who went off again whenever they wanted.[55]

In La Galissonière's day — and it had always been so — the Indians of the Great Lakes could tip the balance as they chose in favour of one or the other of the two powers

that were contending for North America. From the time
of his arrival the alliance with the Indians was more than
just a subject of concern for La Galissonière. Through
the intermediary of the Iroquois or of the English,
news from Europe had always filtered through finally to
these distant tribes. Moreover, the enemy had heaped
necklaces and gifts upon these Indians. Hence their political opportunism. As much as possible they remained
onlookers who let the white men destroy one another.
Only force or their own interests caused them to lean to
one side or the other momentarily. If the price of furs
went up at Oswego or Orange, or the quality of barter
goods improved, nothing could prevent a rush of smuggling in beaver furs towards the Dutch or the English.
The Indian allies behaved in the same way in military
matters. During the recent war the English, as one might
well imagine, had not refrained from spreading through-
out the *pays d'en-haut* the news of the disaster suffered by
the Duc d'Anville's squadron and of their own feats at sea.
According to them they were soon going to drive out of
all the colonies in North America those ambitious Frenchmen and capture their ships and merchandise even before
these reached them. During his long trip along the Ohio
and as far as Detroit Céloron de Blainville was able
to verify the disastrous effects of this news. Almost everywhere the commandants of the forts, who lacked merchandise, had been insulted by over-excited Indians. Quickly
the Indians had gone first from opportunism to hostility,

then to pillaging French canoes and even committing murder.[56]

Immediately after his victory over Sir William Phips, Frontenac had sent a messenger to the West to announce the good news and raise the Indians' morale. Beauharnois and Hocquart had done the same. They sent Louis La Corne, Sieur de Chaptés, François-Josué La Corne Dubreuil, and François-Marie Picoté de Belestre, accompanied by 26 of the principal chiefs of the settled Indians, to the *pays d'en-haut*, not to announce a victory but to try to restore some prestige to the French. These men, who set out on snow-shoes in January 1747, were commissioned to invite all the Great Lakes tribes to come down to Montreal the following spring, with a view "to fighting the common enemy if he dares attempt any undertaking against this colony."[57] Louis La Corne had gone to Detroit, then to Michilimackinac, on foot all the way. He was entirely successful. On 6 July 1747, before La Galissonière's arrival in Canada, he entered Montreal with a band of 250 Indians from all the tribes of the *pays d'en-haut*.[58]

In his policy towards the Indians La Galissonière does not seem to have introduced any innovations. Like his predecessors, he did not conceive of anything beyond a utilitarian policy, one that could be defined as follows: the Indian had to remain a hunter, a supplier of furs in the service of the French, and if need arose, a warrior.[59] This was necessary because the Indian was linked economically

to the life of the colony and because he was a subject of
the king of France. In return for his allegiance to France
the Indian would receive the Christian faith, an element
of civilization which would amend his own; he would also
receive European merchandise, another element of
civilization which would improve his primitive condition.
The Indian would receive his reward for his alliance with
the French above all, thanks to the chain of posts that
surrounded him. These posts and their commandants,
the representatives of French power, would bring him
something precious, something which he would not
always appreciate, and which would sometimes be accompanied by too flagrant acts of exploitation of his weakness or his destitution: peace, the *Pax indiana.* If the
French forts had not been there to maintain order and
security, the Great Lakes country would have become a
true hell. This was why La Galissonière relied upon the
commandants of the posts in his policy towards the
Indians. At the most we see him outline a few projects
concerning the Iroquois. He wanted Abbé François
Picquet to receive aid in his project for an Iroquois mission on the shores of Lake Ontario, near La Galette
(Ogdensburg, NY) and Fort Frontenac (Kingston, Ont.)[60]
He thought it a good idea to create villages round about,
seeing here a possibility of dividing the Indians of the
Iroquois confederacy by rallying to the French cause those
who were converted to the Catholic faith.

2 *A Vigorous Argument*

The official correspondence from the colonial period of the *ancien régime* contains nothing stronger or more inspiring than La Galissonière's arguments in favour of retaining the overseas dependencies. Fully aware of the king's slackness and changeableness of mind and the traditional ultra-conservatism of the ministry of the Marine, he knew that in those high places one encountered, if not a lack of awareness, at least a great deal of inertia on the subject of the colonies. The king was not adverse to his possessions in America, but he would so much have liked colonies that brought in big profits and had not cost anything! In the ministry of the Marine, where every effort was made to concur with the monarch's opinion, nothing was so painful as to have the routine disturbed. That was what La Galissonière attacked.

His arguments are not to be sought only in his official correspondence with Maurepas during his stay in Canada. It was after his return to France that La Galissonière defended the cause of the colonies most vigorously, particularly in his important "Memoire sur les colonies de la France dans l'Amérique septentrionale."[1] The author does not disguise the truth. These colonies, Canada and Louisiana, he admitted, "cost and will cost for a long time far more than they bring in." Canada in particular had always been "a burden on France," and it appeared likely that it would be for a long time. These colonies could not compete with their neighbours in New England on the markets of Europe, or on those of the mother country or in the West Indies. They did not have as many people, nor were they as well equipped. They were not as favourably situated as their rivals on the seaside: the ships of the mother country could not reach them more than once a year. Moreover they had only two routes by which they lived, the St. Lawrence and the Mississippi; a maritime power such as England could easily block these two routes and asphyxiate these colonies.

Nevertheless, it was necessary to come to the aid of the French possessions in North America. In calculations of their profit-earning capacity, not enough account was taken of "the enormous quantity of foodstuffs and manufactured products" that France sent in return for their furs: various kinds of meal, textiles of all sorts, powder, arms, wines, farming and lumbering equipment, all of them articles which kept the mother country's industry and trade going. If these colonies were lost, especially those on the Gulf of St. Lawrence, it would mean the loss of all the French fisheries; the fisheries were "a very lucrative branch of trade" and one on which France's "perpetual enemies" would grow rich. Cod-fishing was also France's best school for sailors. But the principal wealth of Canada, as of the Illinois country, was in the fact that they produced men, "a form of wealth far more precious for a great king than sugar and indigo, or, if one prefers, all the gold of the Indies." He invoked, however, other motives: for example, that the English, who for a century had multiplied their efforts and expenditures to seize them, knew well the great value of Canada and Louisiana. On this point La Galissonière was to be one of the rare administrators who would endeavour to reveal to the French in France what they had so much difficulty in conceiving: that New France was a country on an immense scale. This great and practical dreamer saw here his supreme reason for hope. It was not possible, he said, that such a vast country did not conceal immense riches. He was to come back to this idea twice in his report in 1750. He wrote, for example: "However great the drawbacks set forth in the preceding article, they need not be compared with the future and uncertain proceeds both of Canada and of Louisiana, proceeds which are, however, extremely probable, since they are based upon an immense country, a great people, fertile lands, forests of

mulberry trees [*meuriers*], and mines which have already
been discovered.''[2]

La Galissonière did not lack arguments. With the
mother country he was not afraid to call up considerations
of honour: it was not possible, he maintained, to abandon
to their own resources Frenchmen who had crossed the
seas, had founded a colony, and had always counted on
France for protection, which they deserved because of
their loyalty. He also brought in the religious considera-
tion, which prohibited giving up "so beneficent a work
as that of converting the infidels who inhabit this vast
continent." It is understandable that La Galissonière,
who was above all a soldier, stressed heavily the strategic
value of Canada. He had acquired the conviction that if
England could be defeated, it could only be in Canada.
She could not be vanquished in Europe; it was here that
she was most vulnerable. Canada was "the strongest barrier that can be opposed to the ambitions of the English."
According to his calculations, England's situation in
Europe and her naval forces were such that the French
could not wage war in Europe with any hope of success;
"here, on the contrary, all the natural advantages are on
our side ... and it would cost little to destroy several settlements which are of great value to her and which do much
harm to ours."[3] La Galissonière opportunely recalled that
France's recent great disasters were to be ascribed to her
weakness at sea. Nor could she for a long time hope to be
able to afford a navy equal to the English fleet. What way

out remained for her, then, other than attacking England in her possessions? Such attacks could not, however, be carried out successfully with forces sent out from Europe, even at considerable expense. There was only one solution available: the French must entrench themselves in America. In that way France could save her colonies, and at less cost than with forces fitted out in the mother country.

La Galissonière had uttered the word "expense." Expense! This was the greatest grievance held against the colonies on the St. Lawrence in the offices of the Marine and even at the court. La Galissonière could not overlook this reproach, particularly, as he said, since, as acting governor-general, he was responsible for the extraordinary expenses of recent years, which had been caused by the war.[4] In 1747 the amount of the bills of exchange drawn on the paymasters-general of the Marine for 1746 startled Maurepas. The king himself did not conceal that he was most shocked by it. It was claimed that the whole service of the Marine had been so upset by it that it had been necessary to suspend "essential operations." If, proportionally, the other colonies had caused half as much expense as had Canada, it was said, "there would not have been enough left to fit out a single ship."[5] To understand this question of finances properly it must be kept in mind that under the *ancien régime* in France there was no budget for the colonies. They were included in the budget of the Marine, as were expenditures for the galleys and some other items. This was extraordinary in a country which at that time possessed bigger colonies than anyone else. And since the royal government was niggardly with the budget for the Marine, and since this budget remained the same, even when others were being increased, it is not astonishing that the colonies perpetually received much less than they needed.[6] To the reproaches of Maurepas and the king, La Galissonière first ventured to give a peremptory reply: "In France there are many frontier towns which produce nothing at all, which were, however, built at great cost and are maintained and protected at great expense." In his report of 1750 he added: "Can one give up a country, no matter how poor it is or how much it costs to maintain it, when by its position it confers a great advantage over one's neighbours?"

What was surprising about the fact that expenses had increased considerably in 1746 and 1747, during the war? "The king's orders," Maurepas was reminded by Hocquart, "were not that we should simply remain on the defensive, but that we should take the offensive ..." In actual fact 27 war parties had been sent off in all directions since 1745: into Acadia, into New England, against the Mohawks, towards the Great Lakes, parties that were composed of Indians, militiamen, colonial regular troops.[7] This small-scale warfare had proved to be efficacious. "We have sown consternation among our neighbours," testified Hocquart.[8] These parties had, in addition, saved the alliance of the Indians with the French. If they had not been used, the Indians would have turned against the French. Moreover, it had soon been necessary to prepare for a threatened invasion by the St. Lawrence and Lake Champlain. But was it known at Versailles and Paris how much this sort of war could cost? A visit by La Corne de Chaptes and his group to the various tribes in the *pays d'en-haut*, to rekindle the Indians' trust, had alone cost the treasury 60,000 *livres*.[9] The cost of arming, feeding, and clothing a single Indian amounted to hardly less than 250 *livres* a year. And yet the Indians still found grounds for dissatisfaction and grumbling. It had cost more than 10,000 *livres* merely in necklaces and beads just to induce the settlement Indians to take up the war-song and accept the tomahawk that had been held out to them in 1745. The alliance with the Indians, Hocquart might have pointed out, demanded the top price. But whose fault was that? A decently populated colony could have, at least in good measure, done without these auxiliaries.

La Galissonière took credit to himself for pointing out a way of reducing these expenses which seemed enormous to Maurepas and which upset the whole budget for the Marine. His suggestion was to restore full credit to the playing-card and paper money, then to draw "without any discount or hindrance or formality, a single issue of short-term letters of exchange for everything that would be handed in to the Treasury." According to La Galissonière, if this reform were announced and carried out soon, "without waiting until the month of October," it

would by that same autumn bring about " a considerable
reduction in the price of merchandise from France and of
food produced in Canada, with a consequent reduction
in the King's expenditures, a reduction which would become still greater when it was known that the letters of
exchange had been paid regularly despite this facility."[10]

How would this reform be received? Whatever happened, La Galissonière was facing the minister squarely
with this dilemma: "After all, even if this remedy were
not as advantageous as I hope, we must think of the alter-
native upon which we are going to embark, which is
either to bring about, by whatever means, a drop in the
price of goods and provisions, or to increase the pay of
all persons of all conditions who are in the King's service
in this colony; what would be done would be done for
good, and would have quite different consequences for
His Majesty's finances than what I am proposing to you,
which is only an advance and which would be amply made
up for, perhaps that same year."[11] The dilemma ended
with this conclusion that was even more categorical:
"Furthermore, I am not unaware of the difficulties of
France's finances, and particularly for the Marine in the
present circumstances, but that does not prevent me from
persisting in my opinion."[12]

La Galissonière signed this letter on 24 October 1747,
scarcely five weeks after his arrival. How far removed this
authoritative tone seems from the correspondence, defer-
ential and timid, of Beauharnois and Hocquart and so
many other administrators who had preceded them! This

governor, who was a naval man and who knew his milieu well, spoke as a governor. But one can imagine the effect produced on the other side of the ocean. Never had such an alarm rung out in the drowsy bureaux at home since the distant period of the courageous Jacques-René de Brisay, Marquis de Denonville – and Denonville had spoken as a man who had been driven to resigning.

This justification of expenses, which was simply part of his plea in favour of the colonies, did not lead La Galissonière to forget his crowning arguments. As a heading there might have been inscribed this maxim, believed to come from Richelieu, Louis XIII's minister: "It is not proposed to expatiate upon the usefulness of colonies. There are few people today who do not agree that they are in some way necessary to a great state." La Galissonière insisted upon this truth in his arguments. For him the preservation of New France was essential to the future of North America: if New France collapsed, then all the Spanish possessions would come under the domination of the English. (This did, in fact, take place.) Moreover, he believed that the destiny of France, her prestige and her place in Europe and the world, were at stake in this undertaking: therefore "it is of the greatest importance and absolutely necessary not to neglect any means or spare any expense to assure the preservation of Canada, since it is only in this way that we can succeed in saving America from the ambitions of the English, and since the progression of their empire in this part of the world is what is most capable of giving them superiority in Europe."[13]

How can one fail to discern in these warnings the impatience of a man who believed that he had been sent to repair the errors resulting from a lack of foresight and inertia that had lasted too long, and who, somewhat disillusioned, already saw the treaty of 1763 coming?

3   *A Concerted Policy*

La Galissonière, who was above all a soldier, was to devote his attention primarily to the fortifications of the empire. But he was too intelligent not to realize that a simple line of forts, even though they were set up at pivotal points, would not make up a country. In other words, La Galissonière could not have failed to work out a concerted policy in which all the elements of a society would be found, elements which would assist one another, which would be built in a system of hierarchies. "Great men," claimed Victor Hugo, "are ranked by the dimension of their genius rather than by its kind." The definition would apply to this marquis, whose intelligence took so many varied forms. If time had permitted, we may rest assured that he would have submitted the colony to a policy of complete rebuilding.

It is certain, for example, that La Galissonière saw clearly the importance of agriculture. There is no need to recall how he had visualized each important post, those on Lake Champlain and on the Great Lakes, as centres for clearing land and for farming. In them, the colonist settler would not only have provided for his own needs but would have extended the inhabited portion of the colony, furnished men, backed up the military defence, and been able to share his means of subsistence with possible newcomers. La Galissonière would probably have applied himself to a reform of farming in Canada, to adapting it to the needs of the mother country, which was at that time the essential justification for the existence of every colony. The engineer Louis Franquet would soon be given the task of outlining this reform, which La Galissonnière was not able to do because of the shortness of his administration.

Lumbering, one of the immense resources of the country, did not fail to interest La Galissonière. He was delighted with the situation of Fort Saint-Frédéric and the ease with which help could henceforth be brought to it: "It will, moreover, facilitate the settlements on the land around Lake Champlain and the lumbering operations," he wrote. In the same letter he told the minister of the enlarging of the new ship-building yard at Quebec,[1] where the king had just ordered a new ship.[2] La Galissonière also cast a glance at the ironworks at Saint-Maurice. Qualified technicians were lacking. But, certain of the quality of the ore, he would gladly have undertaken the creation of a foundry "of iron artillery." The guns made in Canada could easily have been exchanged for products from San Domingo and Martinique.[3] La Galissonière ran up against the same obstacle, the lack of technicians, in the operation of salt-works, which would have remedied the regrettable scarcity of salt during the late war. Might he have desired, like Talon, the creation of other industries essential to the colony? He recognized that there did not exist in Canada any "regular industry," but, at the most, certain types of cottage industry. The majority of the country people used up their wool at home. La Galissonière had wondered, like some others, whether it would not have been possible to make cloth or other textiles from the woolly hair of the buffalo in the Illinois country. He made a modest proposal along these lines, which, although it was rather useless, was of a kind to alarm commerce in the mother country. Maurepas did not lose any time in reminding La Galissonière that no industry in the colonies should do harm "to the marketing of industries in France," and that it was important not "to let them multiply."[4]

Because he was absorbed by so many other problems, the acting governor was able to give only a small part of his attention to the colony's trade. In external trade furs continued to be the most important article for export, but the value had greatly decreased. An apparently incurable ill was gnawing away at this trade: smuggling,

which was carried on by the Indians and the French, and
through all possible channels. In large measure this ill
was to be ascribed to the incompetence and niggardliness
of the Compagnie des Indes. The merchandise it im-
ported, particularly its scarlet woollen goods, cost too
much and was inferior in quality to that offered by the
English. Besides, there was always the question: what
method, what means should be used to gather furs?
Should it be by farming out the trade? Should it be by
distributing *congés*? The *congé* was the licence given
to private individuals to go to look for furs at their own
expense. The system of farming out the collection of
furs to the post commandants led to bidding, and consequently to higher prices for merchandise and indeed
to reduction in the quantity of those goods whose price
it was desired to maintain; the result was to anger the
Indians and even the French, who took the road to
Oswego. After reaching an understanding with Hocquart, La Galissonière chose the system of licences. He
hoped that competition between holders of licences in the
same posts would lower the price of goods and calm the
Indians' minds.[5] Anxious to probe further into the
American riddle and open up new fields for supplies of
beaver skins, he encouraged Pierre Gaultier de Varennes,
Sieur de La Vérendrye, in his discoveries.[6]

In another connection, he suggested that a printing
office be set up in Canada, with a view to publishing
ordinances and by-laws.[7]

Finally, let us dwell, if only for a moment, on a field in which we again encounter La Galissonière's overflowing activity. The historian cannot help being moved by the action of this scientist who was so closely associated with the awakening of the intellectual life of a small colonial people. La Galissonière did not start scientific research in New France. It existed before he arrived. Since the time of Louis xiv some minds had been intrigued by it, so that the colony participated, in its humble way, in the excitement which was attracting so many people at that time to the sciences, particularly botany. New France already had interesting and eager searchers.[8] La Galissonière's merit was to enrol for research everyone whom he could mobilize and to give these inquisitive persons a powerful impetus. The traveller Peter Kalm is to be believed when he speaks of La Galissonière's great intellectual qualities and learning, a learning which seemed to him "truly astonishing" and which was concerned with all the sciences. When he listened to him, Kalm thought that he was hearing "another Linnaeus." He depicts La Galissonière asking questions about natural history of all his visitors from remote areas of the colony and particularly from the *pays d'en-haut*. La Galissonière, moreover, had had Jean-François Gauthier, the king's doctor at Quebec, draw up a list of the trees and plants of North America which were worthy of note because of their useful properties. He wanted this list[9] to be sent to all the commandants of forts, especially to those in the West, prescribing that they should collect all sorts of specimens and information on the flora and fauna and minerals in their regions, and even telling how to keep certain specimens of plants, make their observations, and mount collections in these fields. Many of the "curious pieces" discovered by the governor or his searchers were to find their way to his property in France or to the Royal Academy of Sciences, of which he had become an "associate at large."[10] Let us accept another opinion by Kalm: "There has never been and perhaps never will be in Canada a greater patron of science." He was certain that of all the governors and intendants none would inspire such love of science or give such an impulse to research.[11] Doubtless it was not for nothing that the La Galissonières had in the arms of their family three butterflies on a field azure.

4 *The Balance-Sheet of a Government*

How are we to draw up the balance-sheet of this government? Had La Galissonière undertaken too much, had he hoped for too much? Might one at times perceive in his haste to rebuild everything the ruthless will of a dictator? Did he frequently go over the intendant's head? Bigot complained about this: he wrote to the minister that the extraordinary expenses, "which are the main ones, might yet be the less extraordinary if the general did not approve all those which this and that person suggests to him, each one for his own advantage ..." And Bigot added this short sentence: "No one applies to the intendant ..."[1] Was there a certain chimerical streak in La Galissonière? One would be inclined to think so. Who will not see a certain lack of realism in his certainty that it was still possible after 1740 to shut up the powerful English colonies between the sea and the Alleghenies? Just as unrealistic was his desire to overtake the demographic superiority of the English colonies, solely, or almost solely, through the birth-rate of the French settlers and the meagre increase represented by discharged soldiers. Perhaps no less fanciful was the unending line of forts which was to stretch from Niagara to the Ohio and even from Michilimackinac to the Illinois country, and which was to prevent any infiltration by the English or Iroquois into this immense open space. (Was La Galissonière aware of the accurate judgement on this subject expressed by Vaudreuil, who was at the time in Louisiana: that if they withdrew their troops from the frontiers or pulled back the frontiers unduly, they were in danger of losing the Indians' trust and at the same time the little they were trying to hold on to?[2]) Is it possible that La Galissonière had, on the other hand, exaggerated the extent of his influence and authority in the offices of the Ministry of the Marine? Had he believed too firmly in the lucky star of the minister, Maurepas?

If he deluded himself, let us, nonetheless, recognize that La Galissonière thought that he had at hand in Canada a host of men who were equal to his great plans. It is well to take another look at the period when he was in command in New France. From successive generations of poverty-stricken colonists who had been brought up in the harsh school of an immense country and who had no other means of transport but their own legs on land and the strength of their arms on the water, there had been

born in Canada a race of men of iron who were capable of
the most overwhelming tasks, who believed that they were
enriching themselves by widening their horizons, and
who were incapable, besides, of resisting constant adventure, the bewitching appeal of the most distant mirages.
It was a race of walkers and fighters, whom one met one
year in Acadia, Newfoundland, in the Hudson Bay
country, and the following year attacking the English
colonies, somewhere in New England, around the Great
Lakes, in the Illinois country, or in Louisiana.

It is documents such as the "Memoire de Canada de
1747"[3] which show what sort of men a governor of the
period could count upon: energetic officers, who were
also diplomats, capable of restraining or subduing Indians and *coureurs de bois.* There are other reports in
which appear the names of Paul and Joseph de Marin,
Jean-Baptiste Jarret de Verchères, Gilles-Augustin Payan
de Noyan, François-Marie Picoté de Belestre, Jacques
Legardeur de Saint-Pierre, François Lefebvre de Duples-
sis-Faber, Louis-Thomas Chabert de Joncaire, Claude-
Pierre Pécaudy de Contrecoeur, Jacques-Pierre Daneau
de Muy, Pierre Margane des Forêts et de Lavaltrie.
La Galissonière has himself supplied us with some lists
of these great servants in which are mentioned Céloron
de Blainville, Coulon de Villiers, Louis-Antoine Dazmat
de Lusignan, who were present at the engagement at
Minas, and how many others! He would have liked the
worth of these men to be better known in France and

their zeal stimulated with promotions in the military
hierarchy and decorations. "Everyone here is too old for
his rank," he sighed.[4] How highly he valued, along with
others, the Sieur Bertet, who was apparently a model
commandant in the Illinois country and whom he knew
through his letters.[5] He was correct also in his judgement
of Céloron de Blainville, for whom Madame Bégon did
not much care because of his "haughtiness," but who was
"a man made to command," according to Father Bonnecamps, his companion in the long trip down the Ohio.[6]
Céloron, who was the commandant of Detroit, was promoted to the rank of major and at the same time, on La
Galissonière's recommendation, his jurisdiction and prerogatives were extended to take in the posts among the
Illinois, the Miamis of the Cuyahoga River, and the
Ouyatanons and Wabash nations.[7] This was a small empire carved out of the great one. It would seem that so
vast a territory had never been assigned to an official of
the colony.

Did La Galissonière take only this image of the genera-
tion of 1750 to France? Alas, he was present at the in-
auguration of another period, that of Bigot. Before he left
he witnessed the new intendant's display and sumptuous,
extravagant expenditures. So much money was going to
be lost of which the colony might have made much better
use. On seeing the "thousand carts" which carried M.
Bigot's baggage, silverware, mirrors, trinkets, Madame
Bégon exclaimed: "If Monsieur Hocquart had seen that,

I think that he would have died of grief." A passion for festivities seized the little society of Quebec and Montreal. The only subject of conversation was balls, great dinners, dances. Old ladies learned to dance. Others shortened their period of mourning to take part in the gaiety. Members of the Order of Saint-Louis were in the worst state of debasement after too heavy dinners.[8] Like all fashionable societies in the world on the eve of great catastrophes, it seemed that that of New France had decided to try forgetfulness and to lose its head. La Galissonière, who was always very correct in his behaviour, took part in these social events only to the degree required by his rank and functions. Nevertheless, what could he not forecast from these strange excesses? Could he refrain from having sombre forebodings? He was, we know, a man who liked the simple life. He was even pious. During his stay at Montreal he heard mass every morning and never missed an evening service or a feast of devotion. Every day at Montreal he spent a few hours with his aunt Bégon, to relax from his work and his calls in the company of a woman of wit and to play with his aunt's little girl.[9]

La Galissonière tried to save the colony. Why did his attempt, which was energetic and intelligently conceived, fail? There are many reasons. The shortness of his administration accounts for a great deal. He landed at Quebec on 19 September 1747, and his mandate ended on 15 August 1749, when La Jonquière arrived. What were two years, when almost everything had to be done over again? Canada had scarcely had time to realize the treasure that it possessed in the person of this nobleman, wrote Kalm, when it was unfortunate enough to lose him.[10] La Galisonnière's misfortune was also that he had no one to carry on his work. La Jonquière and Ange de Menneville Duquesne, two worn-out men, had administrations as short as his own. Furthermore there was one exceptionally serious question: Could New France still be saved as 1750 approached? Had France from that moment not already lost her possessions in America? One feels that they were lost, and had been for a long time, in the minds of Louis XIV and Louis XV. Yet warnings to Versailles had not been lacking before those of La Galisonnière. Philippe Rigaud de Vaudreuil and Michel Bégon had already written: "Being convinced that the nation in Europe which is master of Canada will subsequently be master of all America, the English have it constantly in mind to become masters of all of North America ..."

To understand correctly the evolution of the king's ideas on this subject, all that is needed is to compare two texts. On 3 November 1666 Talon wrote to Jean-Baptiste Colbert: "Only great enterprises befit great souls like the king's, and nothing ordinary is for minds of the quality of yours." Some twenty years later the Marquis de Denonville was, for his part, to write: "The king of France is not a sufficiently great seigneur to develop such a great country." The sentences point up the policy of grandeur of a monarchy at the height of its power, and the policy of the same monarchy in its decline. In fact, it was not only in La Galissonière's time that Versailles expressed dissatisfaction with the expenses of the colony and exhibited a disturbing indifference towards Canada. Even in Denonville's period Versailles was tired of this colony across the seas. In 1689 M. Jacques-Charles de Brisacier, of the Foreign Missions, recommended peace at any price to his priests, for, he informed them, "people at court are already so tired of Canada that if they knew what goes on there they would perhaps seize the opportunity to abandon it completely. They were very near doing so this year, they debated as to whether the troops should not be withdrawn and sent elsewhere, and, far from sending us more help, they felt that they were doing us a great favour in leaving us what you have; besides, what may we not fear with this change in governors [Frontenac had just been appointed to his second mandate]."[11] In 1696, on the eve of the Peace of Ryswick, Louis XIV wrote to Frontenac and Jean Bochart de Champigny: "His Majesty is obliged to warn them that it does not appear that he can long bear the expense to which the war in Canada is putting him." Three years later the complaint was more alarming: "You must believe that His Majesty can grow tired of a colony that costs him enormous sums every year and whose products, far from being of any profit, cause him to lose immense sums every year."[12] In 1727 the same grievances reappeared. Hocquart was warned that "the expenditures that the king makes in the colony are so great that it is to be feared that His Majesty will not be capable of continuing them."[13]

In France, to tell the truth, neither the court nor the offices of the ministry of the Marine ever understood the incalculable value of the domain that Frenchmen had acquired and prepared for them in North America. Similarly they had not grasped the absolute interdependence of the east and west sections of the empire. Everything seemed too big to them, needlessly big. What was still more serious was that a deep discordance finally developed between the monarchy's policy in Europe and its colonial policy in America, and this discordance lasted too long. While Versailles imagined that England's ambition was assuaged in Europe by the Peace of Aix-la-Chapelle, in America the climate of war persisted and the claims, even the attacks, by the English colonies only became more virulent. The court of Versailles did not want to do or permit anything which might grieve the court of London. This meant that the administrators of New France had their hands tied and felt incapable of any riposte. As we have already said, the Peace of Aix-la-Chapelle did not seem "stupid" only in Europe. In New France it took on the aspect of a second Treaty of Utrecht. It forced the disbanding of all the war parties which were being organized against the enemy to the south, who, for his part, did not fail to profit from this advantage.

We know what an energetic reaction the news of the peace and its consequences provoked in La Galissonière.

Immediately he wrote to the minister, without mincing matters: "Your letters about the treaties have frightened me. The abandonment with which they threaten such a useful and zealous colony is not believable. I am certain that you will not agree to it. These letters bind my arms. By this winter I could have carried out some undertaking against Hudson Bay or Oswego, or against some other post. War is not fought anywhere without expense. I am to be pitied for having been sent to a country full of brave people whom I cannot let act ... If we do not attack, we will be attacked ..."[14] Indeed, holes were opening up everywhere in the colony's thin cuirass, holes which were soon to become yawning and which France refused to block, as the cost seemed enormous. Always the cost! In short, to succeed in his vast projects, La Galissonière would have had to learn the art of working miracles: of doing much with nothing.

5 *A Glorious End to a Career*

Did La Galissonière learn of Maurepas' disgrace before he left Canada? It is possible that the last ships from France had brought the news of his exile from the court in April 1749. La Galissonière must have felt some disillusionment on hearing it. Would Maurepas' successor carry on the reform which had finally been started in the offices of the Marine? La Galissonière left behind him in Canada the unanimous regret of a people and a great memory. Despite her relationship with the Marquis, Madame Bégon's testimony can be believed. Even before La Galissonière's departure she wrote to her son-in-law: "It would be desirable for our country that M. de La Galissonière be left here. I very much doubt that anyone will be appointed who will perform as well as he in all matters: I say this without wanting to flatter him and without any prejudices. You know me, and you know that I am honest, perhaps often too much so ..." On another occasion she wrote: "Every day I have the pleasure of hearing: 'Ah! If the general were still with us and if M. Michel [de Villebois] were intendant, Canada would be fortunate.' " A little later, when she was back in France, Madame Bégon drew the expression of the same regret from the letters that she received from Canada: "All of Montreal and a great part of Quebec are infinitely sorry to have lost M. de La Galissonière."[1] Those who were to study the man and his work a little later and from a distance did not think differently. The Ursulines, who normally were good judges of events in their time, were to remember a "Count" who was "a scholar as well as a soldier." In 1752 Jean-François Gauthier, the king's doctor in New France, gave this testimonial: "The Marquis de La Galissonière is the only person who had begun to put things on a sound footing. In losing him, Canada has suffered a very great loss."[2] The Marquis de Montcalm was no less generous in his praise; speaking in 1757 to a group of Ottawas who had come to congratulate him on the capture of Oswego, he reminded them of "their former father, M. de La Galissonière, who was not large, but who had carried out large things."[3]

Almost as soon as he was back in France La Galissonière became the specialist on colonial matters. At the court, at the ministry of the Marine, he was consulted about the

overseas possessions. In connection with his 1750 "Memoire" there are these significant lines: "In 1751 M. de
La Galissonière, who was worthy of commendation for
his qualities, his knowledge, and his zeal for the honour of
the king and his state, presented a report, of which all the
king's ministers wanted to have a copy, concerning
France's colonies in North America. He had governed in
Canada; he had been in all the colonies in North America; he had studied them and he knew them; he considered Canada to be the bulwark of all the other colonies ..."[4] It is not astonishing, then, that he was assigned
the most important tasks.

Following the Treaty of Aix-la-Chapelle it had been
agreed that plenipotentiaries would set for France and
England the boundaries of the colonies belonging to these
two powers in North America. In France the services of
the Marquis de La Galissonière and Etienne Silhouette
were called upon in 1750. Then began a hard and dis-
appointing piece of work, on which La Galissonière was
to lose some of the best years of his life. Given the state of
rough draft in which the cartography of North America
still stood, and with a rival who was more or less prepared
to admit the truth, what results could the commissioners
hope for? The French delegation had announced its
readiness to discuss the American problem in its entirety,
including claims to the West Indies and the Ohio country.
William Shirley and William Mildmay objected to this

all-inclusive discussion; they intended to limit themselves
to setting out the frontiers of Acadia. In March 1751 the
French delegation was completing a voluminous docu-
mentation on the island of Saint Lucia. A session was held
at that time on the division of the war-time captures, then
there was an adjournment for some months. In 1752 the
negotiations started again. This time there was strong an-
tagonism between Shirley's aggressiveness and Mildmay's
conciliatory policy. France threatened to publish the
text of the discussions and thus alert European opinion.
Angered, England threatened war. Thus ended the
negotiations, which had been started under the illusion
of a possible understanding. From them there remained
reports which attest to the accurate information gathered
by La Galissonière during his short stay in Canada.

The Marquis's career had not, however, stopped its
meteoric climb. In 1750 he was put in charge of the Dépôt
de la Marine, where were stored the log-books, plans, and
maps of the Marine. That same year he was made a com-
modore, then in 1752 he became a commander of the
Order of Saint-Louis, and in 1755 a rear-admiral. The
previous year, when he had been promoted commander
of a squadron of three warships and six frigates, he had
taught naval tactics to the young officers.[5] Then came his
moment of glory.

It was the year 1756. France and her ally, Spain, could
no longer count the number of their defeats at sea and in

the colonies. At sea, however, an ultimate effort was to be made. In the face of the enormous superiority of the English fleet, France succeeded in acquiring some men-at-war. In the Mediterranean, a station threatened the two allies, the island of Minorca, which England was fortifying as best it could. It had made it into a second Gibraltar. Louis xv decided to conquer the fortress. The attack was to be carried out on land and by sea. The troops, 12,000 strong, were entrusted to the Duc de Richelieu. La Galissonière commanded a squadron of 12 men-of-war, 5 frigates, and 150 transports. This was not his first encounter with the English. Earlier, during a voyage to India, he had exchanged gunfire with them at sea and had captured a brigantine from them.[6] After a siege that lasted several weeks, Richelieu succeeded in landing. The besieged came to surrender to La Galissonière, who was in command of the *Foudroyant*. But at that moment the English squadron, commanded by Admiral John Byng, arrived in haste to bring aid to Minorca. It consisted of 13 men-of-war, one of them a three-decker, and 5 frigates. For some days the two admirals manoeuvred, each trying to take advantage of the wind. Finally, on 20 May 1756, the French admiral thought that he was in a favourable position. For four hours he attacked furiously. Byng had to stand out to sea. The anger caused in England by this defeat is well known.

After this exhausting battle the victorious admiral,

whose health was already impaired, felt that he could not
go on. The king called him to Fontainebleau. He attempted to go there. His majesty, it seemed, had a mar-
shal's baton in store for him. But the hero was already
covered with fame. When he landed at Toulon, the
whole population was there to acclaim him, and his
cousin, the Duc de Richelieu. All eyes sought out this
little man who had just beaten the English fleet and had
won "the greatest naval victory of the century"[7] over the
eternal enemy. A salvo of 21 guns was fired in honour of
the two victors.[8] Unfortunately, the admiral died on his
way to the king, at Nemours, on 26 October 1756.[9] He
was only 63 years old. His mind was still bubbling over
with all sorts of plans. The little town of Nemours ac-
corded him a funeral that was in a way a state event. Everyone went to great expense: the musketeers and their
officers who were quartered there, the clergy, the nobility
and the leading citizens, probably some seigneurs from
the court who had come from Fontainebleau, and some
members of his family, paid their final respects to him.[10]

Thus, in the little town of Nemours, ended the fame
which was to surround for only a short time the tomb of
the Marquis de La Galissonière, admiral of France, the
vanquisher of Byng. In 1772, somewhat belatedly, his
family erected a monument over the tomb of this glorious
son of France in the chapel of Saint Joseph in the church
of Saint John the Baptist in Nemours. First, a slab of
black marble marked the exact resting-place of the

deceased; a second slab, of white and red marble, bearing the arms of the family, an "indicatory epitaph" in Latin, and a "summary" of the marquis's life, was affixed to the right wall of the chapel. But the Seven Years' War, the Treaty of Paris, the loss of her colonies which relegated France to the second place in Europe, caused many events and many names in her colonial history to be forgotten. Then came the Revolution, which destroyed the heraldic monuments. Later, when repairs were made in the church, the slab of black marble and the "indicatory epitaph" were moved. The agreements made with the family were resolutely broken. There was even a moment, wrote Emmanuel de Cathelineau, when, "stripped of the marble that covered him, La Galissonière was deprived of any tomb."[11]

A visit to La Galissonière's former *château* leaves an equally melancholy memory. It would have been a happy fortune to see this *château* and its domain preserved. We know that the marquis had built greenhouses for himself, had sown and cultivated seeds of the flora of Canada, had even planted trees there from the great country. Today the traveller would like to look for what has remained of these plants. Of the domain he will only see immense vineyards, through holes in a wall which has fallen down in places. In the middle of these vineyards stands an ivy-covered tower, the top of which has been removed: this is all that remains of a domain that was sold at auction and of a *château* that was put to the torch

in the terrible struggle between republicans and royal-
ists.[12] And how many archives of value to Canada perhaps
went up in flames with the *château*!

On this sad note ends the story of the man who was
perhaps the most intelligent and the most cultivated of
the governors of New France. Pierre Gaxotte has made
the following comment on Dupleix, the great man of
India: "By a humiliating coincidence France, which did
not believe in its colonizing genius, possessed the greatest
supporter of colonial expansion of all times, Jean-
François Dupleix."[13] If Gaxotte had known Roland-
Michel Barrin de La Galissonière better, he would have
paid the same homage to this other "great colonial" of
the *ancien régime*.

NOTES AND BIBLIOGRAPHY

ABBREVIATIONS

AN   Archives Nationales, Paris

ASQ   Archives du Séminaire de Québec

BN   Bibliothèque Nationale, Paris

BRH   *Bulletin des recherches historiques*

COL   Colonies

MSHM   Mémoires de la Société historique de Montréal

NF   *Nova Francia*

PAC   Public Archives of Canada

RAPQ   *Rapport de l'archiviste de la province de Québec*

RUO   *Revue de l'université d'Ottawa*

Notes

INTRODUCTION

1 Bonnault, "La Marquis de La Galissonière," *RUO*, x (1940): 396-407.
2 Ferland, *Cours d'histoire du Canada*, II: 490, 496.
3 Garneau, *Histoire du Canada...*, II: 192.
4 Grandjean de Fouchy, "Éloge de M. le Marquis de La Galissonière," *Histoire de l'Académie royale des Sciences* (Paris, 1762), 147f.; Bezard, *Fonctionnaires maritimes et coloniaux...*, *les Bégon*, 277.
5 Goepp, "Roland-Michel Barrin, marquis de La Galissonière," *BRH* (1902): 122-124; Grandjean de Fouchy, "Éloge," 147; Lamontagne, *La Galissonière et le Canada*, 1.
6 Frégault, *François Bigot*, I: 300f.
7 Grandjean de Fouchy, "Éloge," 148.
8 Cathelineau, "Études sur Roland-Michel Barrin de La Galissonière," *NF*, II: 280.
9 Pageot, *Les amiraux Barrin de La Galissonière et Louis Turpin*, 33f.; Grandjean de Fouchy, "Éloge," 148f.
10 Cathelineau, "Études...," *NF*, II: 280.

11 Beauharnois and Hocquart to the minister, 2 oct. 1739, PAC, C^{11}A, 71: 12-15.

12 Lamontagne, *La Galissonière et le Canada*, 16.

13 The minister to M. de Lestenduère, 9 Dec. 1732, PAC, Series B, 56: 302.

14 The minister to La Galissonière, 6 June, 1747, PAC, C^{11}A, 86-2: 337.

15 *Voyage de Kalm en Amérique*, 183.

CHAPTER 1

1 La Galissonière and Hocquart to the minister, 6 Nov. 1747, PAC, C^{11}A, 87-2: 227f.

2 La Galissonière to the minister, 1 Sept. 1748, PAC, C^{11}A, 91: 109.

3 La Galissonière to the minister, 11 Oct. 1747, PAC, C^{11}A, 87-2: 171-173.

4 *Voyage de Kalm en Amérique*, 184.

5 La Galissonière to the minister, 26 June 1749, PAC, C^{11}A, 93: 139-142.

6 Grandjean de Fouchy, "Éloge de M. le Marquis de La Galissonière," *Histoire de l'Académie royale des Sciences* (Paris, 1762), 149.

7 Mémoire du Roy, 1 April 1746, PAC, Series B, 83: 127-143.

8 Maurepas to La Galissonière and Hocquart, 18 Sept. 1747, PAC, Series B, 85: 147-150. For a detailed account of the encounter at Minas, see the "Journal de campagne de novembre 1746 à octobre 1747," PAC, C^{11}A, 87-1: 37-62.

9 Beauharnois and Hocquart to the minister, 12 Sept. 1745, PAC, C^{11}A, 83 : 3-72.

10 *Ibid.*

11 *Ibid.*

12 *Ibid.*

13 La Galissonière to the minister, 25 July 1749, PAC, C^{11}A, 93: 123-138.

14 *Ibid.*

15 *Ibid.*

16 Letter to Beauharnois, 7 March 1746, PAC, Series B, 83: 91.

17 La Galissonière to Maurepas, 5 Oct. 1748, PAC, C¹¹A, 91:
122-125.

18 La Galissonière, "Memoire" (December 1750,), PAC, C¹¹A, 96:
174-212; reproduced in modern French in Lamontagne, *Aperçu
structural du Canada au XVIII*ᵉ *siècle*, 93-112.

19 La Galissonière to the minister, 26 June 1749, PAC, C¹¹A, 93:
139-142; again, 25 July 1749, *ibid.*, 123-138.

20 Franquet, *Voyages et mémoires sur le Canada*, 172f.

21 La Galissonière and Bigot to the minister, 26 Sept. 1748,
PAC, C¹¹A, 91: 20-23; again, 26 Sept. 1748, *ibid.*, 24-29.

22 La Galissonière to the minister, 21 Oct. 1747, PAC, C¹¹A, 87-2:
198; again, 25 July 1749, *ibid.*, 93: 123-138.

23 La Galissonière to the minister, 25 July 1749, *ibid.*, 93:
123-138.

24 La Galissonière to the minister, 5 Oct. 1748, PAC, C¹¹A, 91:
122-125.

25 M. de Raymond to the minister, 8 Sept. 1748, PAC, C¹¹A, 92:
162-166; La Galissonière to the minister, 5 Oct. 1748, *ibid.*,
91: 116-119.

26 La Galissonière to the minister, 25 Sept. 1748, PAC, C¹¹A,
91: 116-119.

27 Letter from Detroit, 1 Oct. 1732, PAC, C¹¹A, 58: 126f.

28 La Galissonière to the minister, 22 Oct. 1747, PAC, C¹¹A, 87-2:
199f.

29 La Galissonière to the minister, 25 Sept. 1748, PAC, C¹¹A, 91:
116-119.

30 "Memoire" (December 1750).

31 La Galissonière to the minister, 25 Sept. 1748, PAC, C¹¹A,
91: 116-119; La Jonquière and Bigot to the minister, 5 Oct.
1749, *ibid.*, 93: 32-35.

32 Charlevoix, *Histoire ... de la Nouvelle-France ...*, VI: 139f.

33 *Ibid.*, 118f., 139f., 152.

34 Vaudreuil to the minister, 2 Nov. 1748, PAC, C¹¹A, 92: 124-138.

35 "Memoire" (December 1750).

36 La Galissonière to the minister, 1 Sept. 1748, PAC, C¹¹A,
   91: 101-109.

37 La Galissonière to the minister, 26 June 1749, PAC, C¹¹A,
   93: 139-142.

38 *Ibid.*

39 "Memoire" (December 1750).

40 Madame Bégon's correspondence, *RAPQ,* 1934-35: 74.

41 La Galissonière to the minister, 26 June 1749, PAC, C¹¹A,
   93: 139-142.

42 "Relation du voiage de la Belle Rivière fait en 1749 sous les
   ordres de Monsieur de Celoron, par le Père Bonnecamps,
   jésuite," PAC, C¹¹E, 13: 291-331.

43 La Jonquière to the minister, 20 Sept. 1749, PAC, C¹¹A,
   93: 95-105.

44 "Relation du voiage de la Belle Rivière ...," PAC, C¹¹E,
   13: 291-331.

45 La Galissonière to the minister, 25 July 1749, PAC, C¹¹A,
   93: 124-138; quoted in Lamontagne, *Aperçu structural ...,* 52.

46 La Galissonière to the minister, 11 Oct. 1747, PAC, C¹¹A, 87-2:
   167-170.

47 The Chevalier de Bertet died 9 January 1749.
   See La Galissonière to the minister, 26 June 1749, PAC, C¹¹A,
   93: 142.

48 La Galissonière to the minister, 1 Sept. 1748, PAC, C¹¹A,
   91: 101-109.

49 La Galissonière to the minister, 22 Oct. 1747, PAC, C¹¹A, 87-2:
   199f.

50 La Galissonière to the minister, 26 June 1749, PAC, C¹¹A, 93:
   139-142.

51 "Relation du voiage de la Belle Rivière ...," PAC, C¹¹E,
   13: 291-331.

52 Madame Bégon's correspondence, *RAPQ,* 1934-35: 52.

53 "Memoire" (December 1750).

54 La Galissonière to the minister, 25 July 1749, PAC, C¹¹A,
   93: 123-138.

55 "Memoire de Canada de 1747," PAC, C¹¹A, 87-1: 37-62.

56 Letter from La Galissonière and Hocquart, 26 Sept. 1747, PAC,
    C¹¹A, 87-1: 255-270; "Memoire de Canada de 1747,"
    ibid., 37-62.
57 "Journal de campagne de novembre 1746 à octobre 1747,"
    PAC, C¹¹A, 87-1: 37-62.
58 La Corne to the minister, 1 Oct. 1747, PAC, C¹¹A, 89: 190-194.
59 Lamontagne, *La Galissonière et le Canada*, 37.
60 "Memoire" (December 1750).

CHAPTER 2

1 "Memoire" (December 1750).
2 *Ibid.*
3 *Ibid.*
4 La Galissonière to the minister, 24 Oct. 1747, PAC, C¹¹A,
    87-2: 204.
5 Maurepas to Hocquart, 3 April 1747, PAC, Series B, 85: 134f.
6 Maurepas to La Galissonière, 6 March 1748, PAC, Series B,
    87: 177f.
7 Hocquart to the minister, 24 Sept. 1747, PAC, C¹¹A, 88: 9-32.
8 Hocquart to the minister, 27 Oct. 1747, PAC, C¹¹A, 88: 101-112.
9 Hocquart to the minister, 24 Sept. 1747, PAC, C¹¹A, 88: 9-32.
10 La Galissonière to the minister, 24 Oct. 1747, PAC, C¹¹A, 87-2:
    204-210.
11 *Ibid.*, 210.
12 *Ibid.*, 204-210.
13 "Memoire" (December 1750).

CHAPTER 3

1 La Galissonière and Bigot to the minister, 26 Sept. 1748,
    PAC, C¹¹A, 91: 24-29.
2 Maurepas to La Galissonière and Hocquart, 13 Jan. 1748,
    PAC, Series B, 87: 80-82.

3 La Galissonière to Maurepas, 18 Oct. 1748, PAC, C¹¹A, 91 : 154.

4 Maurepas to La Galissonière, 6 March 1748, PAC, Series B, 87: 212.

5 La Galissonière to the minister, 23 Oct. 1748, PAC, C¹¹A, 91: 181-184.

6 Caron, "Pierre Gaultier de Varennes de La Vérendrye ... et ses fils," BRH, XXIII: 171.

7 P.-G. R[oy], "L'imprimerie dans la Nouvelle France," BRH, X: 190f.

8 More about this subject can be found in the pages that I have given in the first volume of my Histoire du Canada français to this soaring of the young Canadian spirit. There are also two well-documented chapters by Roland Lamontagne in his La Galissonière et le Canada, 76-98.

9 This list has been found by Jacques Rousseau. P.-G. Roy, "Le Comte de La Galissonière et la Nouvelle-France," BRH, III: 139.

10 Grandjean de Fouchy, "Éloge," 151.

11 Voyage de Kalm en Amérique, 4-6, 182-185.

CHAPTER 4

1 Bigot to the minister, 8 Nov. 1748, PAC, C¹¹A, 92: 109.

2 Vaudreuil to the minister, 2 Nov. 1748, PAC, C¹¹A, 92: 124-138.

3 "Memoire de Canada de 1747," PAC, C¹¹A, 87-1:37-62.

4 La Galissonière to the minister, 3 Nov. 1747, PAC, C¹¹A, 87-2: 216f., 218-222.

5 La Galissonière to the minister, 1 Sept. 1748, PAC, C¹¹A, 91: 101-109.

6 "Relation du voiage de la Belle Rivière ...," PAC, C¹¹E, 13: 291-331.

7 Maurepas to La Jonquière and Bigot, 14 May 1749, PAC, Series B, 89: 248f.

8 Madame Bégon's correspondence, RAPQ, 1934-35.

9 *Ibid.*, 37, 39, 54.

10 *Voyage de Kalm en Amérique*, 185.

11 Brisacier to Bishop Saint-Vallier, 20 May 1689, ASQ, Lettres, Carton N, 93.

12 *Cahiers de l'Académie canadienne-française*, II: 20.

13 *Ibid.*, 18.

14 *Collection de manuscrits relatifs à la Nouvelle-France*, III: 399f.

CHAPTER 5

1 Madame Bégon's correspondence, *RAPQ*, 1834-35: 61, 69, 147.

2 Quoted by Lamontagne, *La Galissionière et le Canada*; 58; *Les Ursulines de Québec depuis leur établissement jusqu'à nos jours*, II: 319.

3 *Journal du Marquis de Montcalm …*, 216

4 Quoted by Lamontagne, *La Galissionière et le Canada*, 50.

5 Cathelineau, "Études sur Roland Michel Barrin de La Galissonière, *NF*, III: 86; Pageot, *Les amiraux Barrin de La Galissonière et Louis Turpin*, 36f.

6 Grandjean de Fouchy, "Éloge."

7 Bonnault, "Le marquis de La Galissonière," *RUO*, X: 396-407 (*see* note, page 402). It must be added that in 1829 the Council of the Admiralty of France, which had been called upon to choose the sailors who were famous in the reign of Louis XV, included La Galissonière among the most important (*BRH*, II: 58).

8 Cathelineau, "Études," *NF*, II: 277f.

9 Grandjean de Fouchy, "Éloge," 155.

10 Cathelineau, "Études," *NF*, II: 278-280.

11 *Ibid*, III: 84-90.

12 Pageot, *Les amiraux Barrin*, 17f.

13 Gaxotte, *Le siècle de Louis XV*, 240.

Bibliography

I SOURCES

Public Archives of Canada
  AN, Col., Série B, 83, 85-89.
    AN, Col, C¹¹A, 16, 81-86, 87 (ff. 37-62), 88, 89, 91-95, 96
      (ff. 174-212: Memoire sur les Colonies de la France dans
      l'Amérique septentrionale), 97, 99, 107.
    AN, Col., C¹¹E, 13 (Établissement de postes divers, 1665-1756),
      16 (Postes de l'Ouest, 1679-1759).
  BN, MSS, Fr. 22930.
Archives du Séminaire de Québec
  Lettres, Carton N, 93.
Charlevoix, [Pierre-François-Xavier de]. *Histoire et description
  générale de la Nouvelle-France avec le journal historique d'un
  voyage fait par ordre du Roi dans l'Amérique Septentrionale.*
  6 vol. Paris, 1744.
*Collection de manuscrits contenant lettres, mémoires et autres
  documents historiques relatifs à la Nouvelle-France.* 4 vol.
  Québec, 1883-1885.

Franquet, Louis. *Voyages et mémoires sur le Canada.* Québec, 1889.

Grandjean de Fouchy, Jean-Paul. "Eloge de M. le Marquis de La Galissonière," *Histoire de l'Académie royale des Sciences, Année 1756* (Paris, 1762): 147-156.

[Kalm, Peter]. *Voyage de Kalm en Amérique,* edited and translated by L. W. Marchand. MSHM, XVI, XVII (1880).

[Montcalm, Louis-Joseph de]. *Journal du Marquis de Montcalm durant ses campagnes en Canada de 1765 à 1759.* Québec, 1895. Collection des manuscrits du maréchal de Lévis, VII.

Pouchot, M. *Extraits de mémoires sur la dernière guerre de l'Amérique septentrionale, entre la France et l'Angleterre.* Vol. I. Yverdon, 1781.

[Rocbert de La Morandière, Élisabeth (Madame Bégon)]. La correspondance de Madame Bégon, *RAPQ,* 1934-35: 1-277.

Les Ursulines de Québec depuis leur établissement jusqu'à nos jours. 4 vol. Québec, 1863-1866.

II STUDIES

Bezard, Yvonne. *Fonctionnaires maritimes et coloniaux sous Louis XIV. Les Bégon.* Paris, 1932.

Burpee, Lawrence J. *Pathfinders of the Great Plains: A Chronicle of La Vérendrye and his Sons.* Toronto, 1915. Chronicles of Canada, 19.

Bonnault, Claude de. "Le marquis de La Galissonière," *RUO,* X (1940) : 396-407.

Caron, Ivanhoë. "Pierre Gaultier de Varennes de La Vérendrye et ses fils," *BRH,* XXIII (1917) : 171.

Cathelineau, Emmanuel de. "Études sur Roland Michel Barrin de Galissonière," *NF,* II (1927) : 274-283; III (1927) : 32-37, 84-90.

Ferland, J. B. A. *Cours d'histoire du Canada (1534-1759).* 2 vol. Québec, 1882.

Frégault, Guy. *François Bigot, administrateur français.* 2 vol. Montréal, 1948.

Garneau, F.-X. *Histoire du Canada, depuis sa découverte jusqu'à nos jours.* 4 vol. Montréal, 1882.

Gaxotte, Pierre. *Le siècle de Louis XV.* Paris, 1933. Les grandes études historiques.

Goepp, Edouard. "Roland-Michel Barrin, marquis de La Galissonière," *BRH*, VIII (1902): 122-124.

Groulx, Lionel. "La France a-t-elle perdu ou abandonné le Canada ?" *Cahiers de l'Académie canadienne-française,* II (Montréal, 1957): 7-22.

Lamontagne, Roland. *Aperçu structural du Canada au XVIII* siècle.* Montréal, 1964.

– *La Galissonière et le Canada.* Montréal et Paris, 1962.

– *L'Atlantique jusqu'au temps de Maurepas: aspect de géohistoire du Canada.* Montréal, 1965.

Muret, Pierre. *La prépondérance anglaise (1715-1763).* Paris, 1937. Peuples et civilisations, histoire générale, XI.

Pageot, Auguste. *Les amiraux Barrin de La Galissonière et Louis Turpin.* Paris, 1950.

Roy, Pierre-Georges. "Le comte de La Galissonière et la Nouvelle-France," *BRH*, III (1897) : 139.

Index